RECENT EXCAVATIONS IN MONTREAL, CANADA, HAVE BROUGHT TO LIGHT UNDER-
GROUND CONVENT PASSAGES AS MENTIONED IN MARIA MONK'S BOOK

Maria Monk, and Her Revelations of Convent Crimes

HUMAN nature will never be understood by any human being: it baffles us, even when we try to understand ourselves. Those we know best are continually surprising us by some act of which we thought them incapable, or by some assertion which demolishes our belief in their intelligence.

Who would have supposed that a new religion could spring up, in Western New York, base itself upon an absurd fable about golden plates and a new Bible, and then grow to vast power, in spite of contempt, ridicule, and persecution?

Besides the 19th century miracle of Mormonism, the manmade creed of Mohomet is an easy-going achievement, for the Arab merchant imposed upon ignorant nomads, while Joseph Smith and Sidney Rigdon humbugged shrewd, hard-headed, educated Americans.

Who could have supposed that Roman Catholicism would survive the Reformation, reconquer Germany, regain the mastery in Great Britain, and hold the balance of power in the United States, while clinging to the ludicrous dogmas which were almost laughed out of court, at the Renaissance?

Who could have imagined that the proudest intellects of modern Europe could have been submerged by the impudent impostures of fake miracles, fake relics, fake purgatory, fake transubstantiation, fake indulgences, and fake personation of Jesus Christ?

A colossal fraud, a huge anachronism, a standing insult to common sense, is popery, is the worship of Mary, is the purgatorial gold-mine, is the fiction of saints, is the shameless market in which Rome sells *everything*, from a nun's hair to a golden crucifix and a pewter Madonna.

But of all the successful impositions forced upon human credulity by the most arrogant of churches, is that of a virgin priesthood. Unmarried, full-sexed, ruddy and robust with fat living, red of lip and thick of cheek, and dew-lapped of neck, these portly bachelors—thousands of them!—strut up and down the earth, bold-eyed, pretending to sexual purity! And it goes! The brazen fraud is taken for a verity. Not one Catholic

(3)

layman in a thousand doubts that the priest is a man of like passions as himself, but he accepts the fraud, takes the living lie as a necessary evil, considers it bad form to notice anything, and never opens his mouth, unless the priest is so unlucky as to get caught and to cause "scandal."

As to men who are not Catholics, you won't find one in a

FRANCIS DOYLE, FLORIDA PRIEST

million who doubts the real office of the priest's "housekeeper," and the uses to which the jailed women of the nunneries are put, willingly or unwillingly.

But when some individual case challenges the world's attention, when some nun breaks jail and cries piteously for help and protection, *then*, indeed, all the Roman cohorts get into instant action, and the non-Catholics are but too apt to aid the priests in capturing the fugitive and taking her back to the papal Bastille.

In the olden days, there was no such thing as "the escaped nun"—why not? Because, the civil power was wielded by staunch Catholics, and these were compelled by the law of the Roman church to return all such run-aways to the Convent. The penalty for failure to do this, was excommunication, which at that time was well nigh the same as death.

But what were the real conditions of nunneries from the very beginning? As everybody knows, the apostles were mostly married men; the primitive elders and presbyters had wives: and bishops of Rome were married men, during the earlier centuries after Christ. It was not until nearly 1100 years had passed away, that Pope Gregory VII. energetically attempted to enforce celibacy upon the priesthood; and at least 300 years more went by, before its general adoption in the Catholic world. As late as the year 1320, the Irish priests continued to take wives; and the Spanish priests were in full practice, on the same line, in 1335.

Consequently, the thick-lipped, red-faced, rotund and lusty Roman male-Virgin, is a comparatively modern impostor.

(See Lea: History Sacerdotal Celibacy, Vol. 1, pages 365 and 383.)

Let us briefly examine the mode of life which resulted from the unnatural system of confining nuns, in the custody of un-married priests.

A Catholic author writes, "Alas, also, how many priests in their convents have established a sort of infamous gymnasium, where they exercise the most abominable debaucheries." De Planctus Ecclesire, Vol. 11. 2.

Tertullian wrote that the reputation of priests for virginity, covered secret sins "the effect of which were concealed by resort to *infanticide.*"

(Tertull. de Virgin. Veland. C. XV.)

Cyprian's testimony against the male "virgins" was equally sctrong.

Says Dr. Lea, Vol. 1, pages 423 and 244:

"When the desires of man are once tempted to seek, through unlawful means, *the relief denied to them by artificial rules,* it is not easy to control the unbridled passions which irritated by the fruitless attempts at repression, are no longer restrained by a law *which has been broken.*

The records of the Middle Ages are accordingly full of the evidences that *indiscriminate license of the worst kind,* prevailed throughout every rank of the hierarchy.

Scarcely had the efforts of Nicholas and Gregory put an end

to sacerdotal marriage in Rome when the morals of the Roman clergy became a disgrace to Christendom."

In 1130, Cardinal Pier-Leone was elected pope, although he had children by his sister, Tropea, and carried a concubine with him when travelling, as Cardinal Vanutelli is said to have done when he attended the Canadian Council, several years ago.

Pope Innocent VIII. had sixteen illegitimate children, and Pope Alexander VI. nearly as many; and although Pope Benedict IX. was only *ten years old* when made Pontiff by his dissolute mother, he lost no time before sinking into the most swinish debauchery.

Canon Burchard, the private Chamberlain to Pope Alexander VI., wrote:

"The women (of the convents) were persecuted and imprisoned if they had any relation with laymen; but when they yielded themselves to the monks, masses were sung and feasts given. The nuns, thus coupled give birth to gentle and pretty little monks, or else they cause abortions to be performed. If any one were tempted to uphold that this is not true, *he need only search the privy vaults of the convents,* and he will find there nearly as many children's bones as were in Bethlehem in the time of Herod."

(See Human Sexuality, p. 258.)

In describing the morals of the Pope and the priests, the poet Petrarch used language which cannot be printed.

Babylon itself never sunk lower in bestial vice; and Petrarch's feelings were intensified by the brutal assault which the Pope made upon the poet's young and beautiful sister.

Pope Gregory XII. in a letter to an Abbot wrote, in the year 1408:

"Many of the nuns commit fornication with the monks and the lay brothers: and in the same monasteries bring forth sons and daughters * * * and not a few of the nuns destroy the fœtus, and *kill the children who see the light.*"

(Cited, and the full Latin text given in "Nuns and Nunneries," p. 184. See Appendix A to this article.)

The Council of Mayence, under Pope Stephen V., absolutely forbade priests to allow "any description of women to live in the house" with them, and declared that "very many crimes have been committed so that some priests have had children born to them by their own sisters."

(See Appendix B for the Latin decree of the Council.)

Nicholas de Clamenges was a famous Catholic scholar, rector of the University of Paris, in 1393, and later Archdeacon of Baieux. When he died at the College of Navarre, he was buried in the Chapel, under the lamp before the great altar. He published a book on the subject of the corruption in his church. He attributed this evil condition to the vicious lives of the priests, and to the fact that when they committed murder, rape, or any other enormous crime, they can pay themselves out of prison *with money.*

(The Popes had a price-list, and the fine or tax for crimes ranged all the way from theft and gambling up to perjury, incest, sacrilege, assassination, and rape.)

Alluding to other causes of depravity, the Catholic scholar says:

"Touching the Monks and Monasteries, there is abundance of matter to speak of—were it not that it would oppress me to dwell long on the enumeration of so great and so many *abominations.*"

Speaking of the nuns, Clamenges says:

"Modesty forbids me to say much concerning them that might be said." Then he compares the convents to "brothels" and the nuns to "harlots," lewd and incestuous.

In 1774, Duke Leopold of Tuscany investigated the nunneries of his dominions. He was a Catholic, of course, and his main assistant in overhauling the convents was the Catholic Bishop Ricci.

I regret that space cannot be given to all the testimony secured by Duke Leopold and presented in substance to the Pope, but the following passage which occurs in a letter from Bishop Ricci to Cardinal Corsini, sufficiently indicates the conditions uncovered:

"In writing to the Pope, I would not enter into *infamous details which would horrify you.*

Yet what have not these wretched Dominican Monks been guilty of!

The stories of the wife of the Provincial and the mistress of the Confessor, and other follies of like kind, are revolting to every one.

That which I have learned, makes me shudder."

Duke Leopold having become Emperor of Austria, the good Bishop Ricci was left helpless against the monks whom he had exposed and infuriated. The Pope turned against him, he lost his bishopric, and he was compelled to humble himself by signing a recantation of the charges he had made against the licentious monks—charges based upon the sworn evidence of the nuns, and of a number of workmen who had witnessed many of the carousals in the convents.

The immortal Florentine monk, Savonarola, said "The women in the convents are worse than the courtesans"; and the most illustrious literateur the Catholic Church ever produced, told the Pope practically the same thing. Erasmus, in his wonderful book, "The Praise of Folly," lashes the monks and the priests with unsparing severity, nor does he spare the Popes themselves. In his letter to the Prothonotary of Leo X., he enters into frightful details, which, however, were not likely to shock a pontiff who was a chronic sufferer from syphilis.

HANS SCHMIDT, THE PRIEST WHO MURDERED HIS
MISTRESS IN NEW YORK

"There are monasteries where there is no discipline and which are worse than brothels.

There are others again, where the brethren are so sick of the imposture, that they keep it up only to deceive the vulgar.

The convent at best is but a miserable bondage, and if there be outward decency, a knot which cannot be loosed may still be fatal to soul and body.

"Young men are fooled and cheated into joining these orders. Once in the toils, they are broken in and trained into

Pharisees. They may repent, but the Superiors will not let them go, *lest they should betray the orgies which they have witnessed,* They crush them down with scourge and penance, the secular arm, chanceries and dungeons. Nor is this the worst. *Cardinal mateo* said at a public dinner, before a large audience, naming place and persons, *that the Dominicans had buried a young man alive whose father demanded his son's release.* A Polish noble who had fallen asleep in a church, *saw two Franciscans buried alive;* yet these wretches call themselves the representatives of Benedict and Basil and Jerome.

A monk may be drunk every day. *He may go with loose women secretly or openly.* He may waste the Church's money on vicious pleasures. He may be a quack or a charlatan, and all the while be an excellent brother and fit to be made an abbot; while one who, for the best of reasons lays aside his frock, is howled at as an apostate. Surely the true apostate is he who gives into sensuality, pomp, vanity, the lusts of the flesh, the sins which he renounced at his baptism. All of us would think him a worse man than the other, if the commonness of such characters did not hide their deformity. *Monks of abandoned lives notoriously swarm over Christendom."*

(Life and Letters of Erasmus, 175.)

In the "Familiar Colloquies" of Erasmus, there are two which give a racy, vivid outline of the lives of the monks and the priests—the dialogue entitled "The Franciscans," and that between the "Abbot and the Learned Woman."

Chapter VII. of Dr. John W. Draper's "Intellectual Progress of Europe" should be read carefully by those who wish to know what English history reveals, of the natural consequences of trying to compel priests and nuns to live unnatural lives. Nature *will* assert itself.

When Pope Innocent III. authorized Morton, Archbishop of Canterbury, to investigate the condition of the English convents and monasteries, in 1489, it was found that they were hotbeds of sensuality, vices and crimes.

(See Lea: Sacerdotal Celibacy, Vol. II., p. 16.)

In fact, the Popes so thoroughly understood the necessities of nature, in the case of the lusty priest, that a very moderate fine was levied upon the delinquent in the Taxes of the Penitentiary. For the sum of four *gros tournois,* or less than half a florin, the adulterous or concubinary priest could purchase forgiveness of his venial sin.

Perhaps the most infamous book ever printed is that in which the Popes—Vicars of Christ!—jotted down the prices to be paid by criminals of all degrees for the papal pardon of all sorts of crime.

(A copy of this book is in the British Museum.)

Are the nuns free to leave the convents? Are these most pitiable women the slaves of the priests, walled up in a living tomb, utterly without means of resistance and of escape? Are they completely in the power of the priests, and have they any chance whatever to appeal to the State?

Read the decree of the Council of Trent, enjoining all bishops to enforce the close confinement of nuns, by every means, and even to engage the assistance of the secular arm for that purpose.

All Princes are commanded to protect the convent enclosure, and all civil magistrates are threatened with excommunication, if they fail to aid the bishop in throwing the escaped nun back into the living tomb.

God in Heaven! These ravening wolves of Rome have 58,-000 American women now imprisoned, under lock and key, and the State does not dare to exercise the sovereign right to investigate the condition of those cesspools of priestly vice. On the contrary, when some poor, half-maddened girl or woman *does* elude the vigilance of the papal guards, and escape over the dungeon wall, policemen, sheriffs, constables and bailiffs are swift to seize her and drag her back to life-long captivity.

No Catholic woman, it would seem, can reach the pinnacle of religious bliss, until she walks into a papal Bastille, and lets the unmarried priest turn the key on her.

"Spouse of Christ!"—the most loathsome phrase that ever was invented to cover a secret system of hideous pollution.

In a letter to Bishop Ricci, a Paulist monk describes the Portuguese convents as follows:

"The regular priests have become the bonzes of Japan, and the nuns the disciples of Venus. *Their convents were seraglios for the monks."*

In 1851, Dr. Theodore Dwight, of New York, published a book entitled "The Roman Republic of 1849, with Accounts of the Inquisition, and the Seige of Rome."

On page 210, the author says:

"The Republican government having been made acquainted with all the infamous practices among the monks of La Maddalena, and certain Jesuit nuns, who had charge of educating the female foundlings, turned them both out. The Pope (Pius IX.) ordered the monks to be restored, that they might again tyrannize over those unhappy women.

On hearing of this order, the nuns (three or four hundred) exclaimed with one voice, *'We will not AGAIN be the priests' concubines!'* "

The author then relates how the desperate women attempted to save themselves from their former fate by barricading the doors, arming themselves with such poor weapons as the kitchen afforded,—knives, forks, spits, etc.—displayed the Republican flag, and fought off their assailants for two days.

Who were the asailants of these Italian Catholic women that were resisting the Pope's order, which meant renewed sexual submission to the bestial priests?

Those asasilants were French Catholic soldiers, commanded by the old Napoleonic marshal, Oudinot; and these foreign bayonets had been sent into Italy, at the urgent instance of Pius IX., by Napoleon III., whose bigoted Spanish wife was the tool of the Jesuits, and the Evil Genius of France.

The distracted nuns were of course subdued, some of them thrown into lunatics' cells, and the others put under lock and key—the monks being the goalers. What happened *then*, to those women, behind those locked doors and thick walls? God knows.

Blanco White says in his· "Evidences Against Roman Catholicnsm," that during the brief existence of the liberal government in Spain, in 1822, the nuns were offered their freedom, and that in Madrid more than two hundred immediately fled the convents.

Against the monks, in their horrible abuse of the nuns, no witness bore weightier testimony than the ex-monk, Blanco White; and Cardinal Newman himself admitted that the word of White could not be doubted: his character was too lofty and spotless for even the vituperous tongues of mendacious priests.

On page 144 of the work already named, Blanco White says of female convents—"I cannot find tints sufficiently dark and gloomy to portray the miseries which *I have witnessed* in their inmates.

Crime, indeed, makes its way into those recesses, in spite of the spiked walls and prison gates.

This I know with all the certainty which the self-accusation of the guilty can give. In vain does the law of the land stretch a friendly hand to the repentant victim: the unhappy *slave* may be dying to break her fetters!"

But suppose some poor Maria Monk *does* elude her jailers and escape into the world?

White paints the picture of the sickening consequences:

"Her own parents would disown her; friends would shrink from her; she would be haunted by priests and their zealous emissaries, and, like her sister victims of superstition in India, be made to die of a broken heart, if she refused to return to the burning pile from which she had fled in frantic fear."

Of course, Blanco White here refers to the Hindoo *suttee* which required the widow of a Brahman to be burned on the same funeral pyre which consumed the corpse of her husband. Long ago, the English prohibited the *suttee,* and it is now a thing of the past; but what must be the cynical reflections of the learned Brahman when he sees how the English—in the Old World and the New—have allowed the Roman superstition to expand and perpetuate a hideous system of *man's inhumanity to women,* in the lifelong, hopeless and helpless incarceration of duped "Spouses of Christ?"

Blanco White testified to what he saw! Cardinal Newman asserts that Blanco White is to be implicitly believed whenever he states things which he claimed to know. Could evidence be more convincing?

Not a soul ever undertook to overthrow the evidence of this ex-monk of Spain, the tutor in the home of Archbishop Whateley, the Oxford scholar, and the honored friend of the most eminent Englishmen of his day.

So much, then, by way of historic background for the "Awful Disclosures of Maria Monk." We have seen what Popes and Councils alleged against the unnatural life of convents and monasteries; we have seen how the Council of Trent virtually decreed that the nuns were prisoners who must be flung back into their dungeons, if they should escape; we have seen how the roof was lifted off the system by *official investigation,* in Italy and England; we have seen how the Catholic authors—Erasmus, Savonarola, Ricci, and Clamenges—corroborated Luther, Calvin and Knox; we have seen how, in the most modern developments as in the most ancient, the fruits of *the system* are absolutely the same; and we have brought the evidence down to 1849, a date *later* than those involved in the narrative of Maria Monk.

CELIBACY FORBIDDEN BY THE BIBLE.

Not only were the priests of ancient Jewry free to marry, but they were required to do so—for the same decently prudential reasons which demand that a Greek Catholic pastor shall have a wife.

Naturally, therefore, the first Christian ministers were married men, since they were Jews who based their faith in part upon the Old Testament.

Eusebius, in his Ecclesiastical History, states that *Paul, the Apostle to the Gentiles, was a married man!*

Of course every one is aware of the fact that Eusebius is "the Father of Church History," and that he flourished in the time of the Roman Emperor, Constantine the Great. My copy of his work was published in London, in the year 1636.

On page 51, chapter 27, we read—

"Clemens whose words lately we alleged, afterwards reciteth the Apostles which lived in wedlock, *against them which rejected marriage,* saying—

What? do they condemn the Apostles? *for Peter and Philip employed their industry to the bringing up of their children.* Philip also gave his daughter to marriage.

And Paul in a certain Epistle sticked not *to salute his wife,* which therefore he led not about, that he might be the readier unto ministration."

The faces of ancient anchorites, as shown in historical pictures, really look like those of ascetics: they are thin, careworn, devotional, introspective. Apparently, they lived hard and misanthroped a great deal. Their daily diet was bred and water. They wore hair-cloth garments, whipped themselves severely, slept on the bare stones, and ran foot-races with the Devil whenever they felt him heating up their carnalities.

They avoided women, and were afraid to have a piece of calico about. When their thoughts wandered into forbidden paths, they crossed themselves vigorously, and yelled, "Get thee behind me, Lucifer!"

Wine they dared not drink, lest it loosen the bands of self-restraint.

Meat they dared not eat, lest it create red blood of a rebellious nature.

Warm bed clothing they dared not use, lest it invite sensuous dreams to the midnight couch.

Thus they lived abstemiously, mortifying the flesh, rejecting all the good things of nature, and glorifying God, by scornfully refusing to live in accordance with the innate promptings of the sex.

Before a human being of sound mind can be educated into that sort of a monstrosity, he has to be caught early in youth, and carefully trained for the unnatural part.

These olden saints have long since disappeared from earth. The modern Virgins of the Roman Church are built on different lines, and live in a wholly different way. They believe in all the good things that bountiful Nature has provided. They glorify God by having a joyous time.

They find that the allotted span of life is entirely too short to be spent on parched corn and well-water. The whipcord and the hair-shirt, are unknown to their philosophy.

14

In all of their religious papers, you will find the advertisements of the very best wines, made specially for the use of the Virgins, and sold especially to them.

In all of their religious papers, you will find these male Vir-

CARDINAL BILLY O'CONNELL, A MODERN VIRGIN. PICTURE TAKEN
JUST AFTER HE HAD FED SPARINGLY ON DRY
HERBS AND STALE WATER.

gins advertising for feminine "housekeepers," and you will find where the women who wish to keep house for the bachelor priests, advertise their willingness.

At middle age, these modern male Virgins of Rome are

almost invariably corpulent, sensual, gross; with thick, red lips, with dew-lap necks, with bulging eyes, and with swelling abdomens.

As a class, the Roman Catholic priests of today are the most libertine-looking men on earth, and their looks tell a true tale.

As a class, they are EPICURES AND LIBERTINES.

Dr. Justin D. Fulton's dynamic book, "Why Priests Should Wed," reveals the fact that this same Pope Pius IX. authorized, in 1866, a secret order within the priesthood, *as a substitute for marriage.*

That secret order, within the secret orders, *licenses the priests of approved standing to cohabit sexually with nuns who can be relied on to hide the sin.*

Dr. Justin D. Fulton was a responsible and fearless man. He made his damning accusation in a book which Rome has never dared to challenge.

The book was submitted to Anthony Comstock, Post-Office Inspector, before it was given to the printers.

That terrible arraignment of the bachelor priests and their concubines—the cloistered nuns—far surpasses in detail and direct description anything that I ever wrote.

Yet the men whom Dr. Fulton accused never dared to hale *him* to court.

Nor have they ever in any of their papers, pamphlets, books, or sermons denied, THAT POPE PIUS IX. IN 1866, AUTHORIZED PRIESTS AND NUNS TO COHABIT, AS MAN AND WIFE!

Under the administration of the bloated brute, Cardinal William O'Connell, a priest of the name of Pertrachi, notorious for his crimes against Catholic women, was put in charge of the Roman parish at Milford, Mass. He had been several times removed from former appointments because of his unbridled lusts. At Milford, he seized a Catholic woman while she knelt at the altar-rail, alone, feeling secure in the sanctity of the Cathedral. The priest crept upon her from his "sacristy," seized her, dragged her into his private room, *and raped her!*

What was done about it? Nothing. He was never even arrested. He "disappeared," just as John Holtgreve, the Louisiana priest, disappeared from Iberville, after he was indicted for sodomy, committed on the little choir-boys of his church.

The woman whom Petrarchi outraged, *in the Catholic Cathedral,* sued Bishop Beaven for damages, alleging that *he knew* the bad character of the priest, at the time the pastorate of Milford was bestowed upon him.

The case went to the Supreme Court of Massachusetts, where the woman lost, because the Court held that, although Bishop Beaven knew beforehand that the priest would commit the sexual crime with the Catholic women in his charge, the Bishop could not foresee that the priest would *rape* any of them!

(That decision appears in the South-Eastern Reporter, under the case-name of Beaven v Carini.)

TWO MORE AMERICAN VESTALS..... THEY NEVER TOUCH MEAT, OR WINE.

PART 2.

"In the year 1835, Maria Monk was found alone and in a wretched and feeble condition, on the outskirts of New York City, by a humane man, who got her admitted into the hospital at Bellevue. She then told the story in outline, which she afterwards and uniformly repeated in detail, and which was carefully written down and published in the following form: She said she was a fugitive nun from the Hotel Dieu of Montreal, whence she had effected her escape, in consequence of cruelty which she had suffered, and crimes which were there committed by the Romish priests, who had the control of the institution, and to which they had access, by private as well as public entrances. Having expressed a willingness to go to that city, make public accusations, and point out evidences of their truth in the convent itself, she was taken thither by a resolute man, **who afterwards suffered for an act of great merit**; but she was unable to obtain a fair hearing, apparently through the secret opposition of the priests. She reurned to New York, where her story was thought worthy of publication, and it was proposed to have it carefully written down from her lips, and published in a small pamphlet. Everything she communicated was, therefore, accurately written down, and, when copied out, read to her for correction."

The above extract is taken from the Preface to the original edition of "Maria Monk."

It is not my purpose to repeat the story of this unfortunate victim of the Roman *system*. It is practically the same as that of the Italian nuns of 1849; of the Spanish nuns whose fate was indicated by the unimpeachable Blanco White; of the Tuscan nuns who testified before the Commission of Duke Leopold; and of the French nuns who escaped about the same time that Maria Monk did, and whose cases came before the French courts.

(See History Auricular Confession, by Count C. P. DeLasteyrie. Also, "Nunneries," by Seeley.)

In short, Maria Monk, a Canadian girl, entered the Montreal convent in good faith, and soon discovered that she was a prisoner, a slave, a sexual victim of the priests: that if the nuns rebelled, they were barbarously punished, and even killed; that the virginal nuns who resisted the priests were ravished; that infants born in the convent were first baptized and then smothered—just as Pope Gregory XII. charged in his official letter, whose original Latin you will find in the appendix to this article.

Maria Monk gave the following account of herself:

My parents were both from Scotland, but had been resident in Lower Canada some time before their marriage, which took place in Montreal; and in that city I spent most of my life. I was born at St. John's, where they lived for a short time. My father was an officer under the British Government, and my mother has enjoyed a pension on that account ever since his death.

According to my earliest recollections, he was attentive to his family; and a particular passage from the Bible, which often occurred to my mind in after life, I may very probably have been taught by him, as after his death, I do not recollect to have received any religious instruction at home; and was not even brought up to read the scriptures; my mother, although nominally a Protestant, not being accustomed to pay attention to her children in this respect. She was rather inclined to think well of the Catholics, and often attended their churches. To my want of religious instruction at home and the ignorance of my Creator, and my duty, which was its natural effect, I think I can trace my introduction to convents, and the scenes which I am to describe in this narrative.

When about six or seven years of age, I went to school to a Mr. Workman, a Protestant, who taught in Sacrament street, and remained several months. There I learned to read and write, and arithmetic as far as division. All the progress I ever made in those branches was gained in that school, as I have never improved in any of them since.

A number of girls of my acquaintance went to school to the nuns of the Congregational Nunnery, or Sisters of Charity, as they are sometimes called. The schools taught by them are perhaps more numerous than some of my readers may imagine. Nuns are sent out from that convent to many of the towns and villages of Canada to teach small schools; and some of them are established as instructresses in different parts of the United States. When I was about ten years old, my mother asked me one day if I should not like to learn to read and write French; and I then began to think seriously of attending the school in the Congregational Nunnery. I had already some acquaintance with that language, sufficient to speak it a little, as I heard it every day, and my mother knew something of it.

I have a distinct recollection of my first entrance into the Nunnery; and the day was an important one in my life, as on it commenced my acquaintance was a Convent. I was conducted by some of my young friends along Notre Dame street till we reached the gate. Entering that, we walked some distance along the side of a building towards the chapel, until we reached a door, stopped, and rung a bell. This was soon opened, and entering, we proceeded through a long covered passage till we took a short turn to the left, soon after which we reached the door of the schoolroom. On my entrance, the Superior met me, and told me first of all that I must always dip my fingers into the holy water at her door, cross myself, and say a short prayer; and this she told me was always required of Protestants as well as Catholic children.

There were about fifty girls in the school, and the nuns professed to teach something of reading, writing, arithmetic, and geography. The methods, however, were very imperfect, and little attention was devoted to them, the time being in a great degree engrossed with lessons in needlework, which was performed with much skill. The nuns had no very regular parts assigned them in the management of the schools. They were rather rough and unpolished in their manners, often exclaiming, "c'est un menti" (that's a lie), and "mon Dieu" (My God), on the most trivial occasions. Their writing was quite poor, and it was not uncommon for them to put a capital letter in the middle of a word. The only book on geography which we studied, was a catechism of geography, from which we learnt by heart a few questions and answers. We were sometimes referred to a map, but it was only to point out Montreal or Quebec, or some other prominent name, while we had no instruction beyond.

It may be necessary for the information of some of my readers to mention that there are three distinct Convents in Montreal, all of different kinds; that is, founded on different plans, and governed by different rules. Their names are as follows:

1st. The Congregational Nunnery.

2nd. The Black Nunnery, or Convent of Sister Bourgeoise.

3d. The Grey Nunnery.

The first of these professes to be devoted entirely to the education of girls. It would require, however, only a proper examination to prove that, with the exception of needlework, hardly anything is taught excepting prayers and the catechism; the instruction in reading, writing, etc., in fact, amounting to very little, and often to nothing. This Convent is adjacent to that next to be spoken of, being separated from it only by a wall. The second professes to be a charitable institution for the care of the sick, and the supply of bread and medicines for the poor; and something is done in these departments of charity, although but an insignificant amount, compared with the size of the buildings and the number of the inmates.

The Gray Nunnery, which is situated in a distant part of the city, is also a large edifice, containing departments for the care of insane persons and foundlings. With this, however, I have less personal acquaintance than with either of the others. I have often seen two of the Grey nuns, and know that their rules as well as the Congregational Nunnery, do not confine them always within their walls, like those of the Black Nunnery. These two Convents have their common names (Black and Grey) from the colors of the dresses worn by their inmates.

In all these three Convents, there are certain apartments into which strangers can gain admittance, but others from which they are always excluded. In all, large quantities of various ornaments are made by the nuns, which are exposed for sale in the Ornament rooms, and afford large pecuniary receipts every year, which contribute much to their incomes. In these rooms visitors often purchase such things as please them from some of the old and confidential nuns who have the charge of them.

From all that appeals to the public eye, the nuns of these Convents are devoted to the charitable objects appropriate to each, the labor of making different articles, known to be manufactured by them, and the religious observances, which occupy a large portion of their time. They are regarded with much respect by the people at large; and now and then when a novice takes the veil she is supposed to retire from the temptations and troubles of this world into a state of holy seclusion, where by prayer, self-mortification, and good deeds, she prepares herself for heaven. Sometimes the Superior of a Convent obtains the character of working miracles; and when such a one dies, it is published throughout the country, and crowds throng the Convent, who think indulgences are to be derived from bits of her clothes or other things she has possessed; and many have sent articles to be touched to her bed or chair, in which a degree of virtue is thought to remain. I used to participate in such ideas and feelings, and began by degrees to look upon a nun as the happiest of women, and a Convent as the most peaceful, holy, and delightful place of abode. It is true, some pains were taken to impress such views upon me. Some of the priests of the Seminary often visited the Congregational Nunnery and both catechised and talked with us on religion. The Superior of the Black Nunnery, adjoining, also, occasionally came into the school, · enlarged on the advantages we enjoyed in having such teachers, and dropped something now and then relating to her own Convent, calculated to make us entertain the highest ideas of it, and to make us sometimes think of the possibility of getting into it.

Among the instructions given us by the priests some of the most pointed were those directed against the Protestant Bible. They often enlarged upon the evil tendency of that book, and told us that but for it many a soul now condmned to hell, and suffering eternal punishment, might have been in happiness. They could not say anything in its favor; for that would be speaking against religion and against God. They warned us against it, and represented it as a thing very dangerous to our souls. In confirmation of this, they would repeat some of the answers taught us at catechism, a few of which I will here give. We had little catechisms ("Le Petit Catechism") put into our hands to study; but the priests soon began to teach us a new set of answers, which were not to be found in our books, and from some of which I received new ideas, and got, as I thought, important light on religious subjects, which confirmed me more and more in my belief in the Roman Catholic doctrines. These questions and answers I can still recall with tolerable accuracy, and some of them I will add here. I never have read them, as we were taught them only by word of mouth.

Q. Why did not **God** make all the commandments?

A. Because man is not strong enough to keep them.

Q. Why are men **not** to read the New Testament?

A. Because the mind of man is too limited to understand what God has written.

There was a little girl thirteen years old whom I knew in the school, who resided in the neighborhood of my mother, and with whom I had been familiar. She told me one day at school of the conduct of a priest with her at confession, at which I was astonished. It was of so criminal and shameful a nature, I could hardly believe it, and yet I had so much confidence that she spoke the truth, that I could not discredit it.

She was partly persuaded by the priest to believe that he could not sin, because he was a priest, and that anything he did to her would sanctify her; and yet she seemed doubtful how she should act. A priest, she had been told by him, is a holy man, and appointed to a holy office, and therefore what would be wicked in other men, could not be so in him. She told me that she had informed her mother of it, who expressed no anger, nor disapprobation, but only enjoined it upon her not to speak of it; and remarked to her, that as priests were not like other men, but holy, and sent to instruct and save us, whatever they did was right.

I afterwards confessed to the priest that I had heard the story, and had a penance to perform for indulging a sinful curiosity in making inquiries; and the girl had another for communicating it. I afterward learned that other children had been treated in the same manner, and also of similar proceedings in other places.

Indeed, it was not long before such language was used to me, and I well remember how my views of right and wrong were shaken by it. Another girl at the school, from a place above Montreal, called the Lac, told me the following story of what had occurred recently in that vicinity. A young squaw, called La Belle Marie (pretty Mary), had been seen going to confession at the house of the priest, who lived a little out of the village. La Belle Marie was afterwards missed, and her murdered body was found in the river. A knife was also found, covered with blood, bearing the priest's name. Great indignation was excited among the Indians, and the priest immediately absconded, and was never heard from again. A note was found on his table addressed to him, telling him to fly if he was guilty.

It was supposed that the priest was fearful that his conduct might be betrayed by this young female; and he undertook to clear himself by killing her.

These stories struck me with surprise at first, but I gradually began to feel differently, even supposing them true, and to look upon the priests as men incapable of sin; besides, when I first went to confession, which I did to Father Richards, in the old French church ((since taken down), I heard nothing improper; and it was not until I had been several times, that the priests became more and more bold, and were at length indecent in their questions and even in their conduct when I confessed to them in the Sacristie. This subject I believe is not understood nor suspected among Protestants; and it is not my intention to speak of it very particularly, because it is impossible to do so wthout saying things both shameful and demoralizing.

I will only say here, that when quite a child, I had from the mouths of the priests at confession what I cannot repeat, with treatment corresponding; and several females in Canada have recently assured me that they have repeatedly, and indeed regularly, been required to answer the same and other like questions, many of which present to the mind deeds which the most iniquitous and corrupt heart could hardly invent.

At length I determined to become a Black nun, and called upon one of the oldest priests in the Seminary, to whom I made known my intention.

The old priest to whom I applied was Father Rocque. He is still alive. He was at that time the oldest priest in the Seminary, and carried the Bon Dieu (Good God), as the sacramental water is called. When going with a man before him, who rang a bell as a signal to administer it in any country place, he used to ride. When the Canadians, whose habitations he passed, heard it, they would come and prostrate themselves to the earth, worshipping it as God. He was a man of great age, and wore large curls, so that he somewhat resembled his predecessor, Father Roue. He was at that time at the head of the Seminary. This institution is a large edifice situated near the Congregational and Black Nunneries, being on the east side of Notre Dame street. It is the general rendezvous and centre of all the priests in the District of Montreal, and, I have been told, supplies all the country with priests as far down as Three Rivers, which place, I believe, is under the charge of the Seminary of Quebec. About one hundred and fifty priests are connected with that of Montreal, as every small place has one priest, and a number of larger ones have two.

Father Rocque promised to converse with the Superior of the Convent, and proposed my calling again, at the end of two weeks, at which time I visited the Seminary again, and was introduced by him to the Superior of the Black Nunnery. She told me she must make some inquiries, before she could give me a decided answer; and proposed to me to take up my abode a few days at the house of a French family in St. Lawrence suburbs, a distant part of the city. Here I remained about a fortnight; during which time I formed some acquaintance with the family, particularly with the mistress of the house, who was a devoted Papist, and had a high respect for the Superior, with whom she stood on good terms.

At length, on Saturday morning about 10 o'clock, I called and was admitted into the Black Nunnery, as a novice, much to my satisfaction, for I had a high idea of a life in a Convent, secluded, as I supposed the inmates to be, from the world and all its evil influences, and assured of everlasting happiness in heaven. The Superior received me, and conducted me into a large room, where the novices (who are called in French Protulantes), were assembled, and engaged in their customary occupation of sewing.

Here were about forty of them, and they were collected in groups in different parts of the room, chiefly near the windows; but in each group was found one of the veiled nuns of the Convent, whose abode was in the interior apartments, to which no novice was to be admitted. As we entered, the Superior informed the assembly that a new novice had come, and she desired any present who might have known me in the world to signify it.

Two Miss Fougnees, and a Miss Howard, from Vermont, who had been my fellow-pupils in the Congregational Nunnery, immediately recognized me."

This much of Maria Monk's narrative is given in order that it may be seen how definitely she mentions places, names, and events, and how fearlessly she opens the widest door to denial and refutation. She does not talk like the maker of a myth, but with the plain straight-forwardness of one telling a true tale.

When her dynamic book came from the press of Harper Brothers, it was almost as eagerly read as was the New Testament of Erasmus, and the German Bible of Luther. A profound, national sensation was felt. Even in England, the Romanists quaked at the consequences of these fearful revelations.

The priests denied that Maria Monk had ever been a nun; then they alleged that she *had* been one, but had been expelled because she was *bad;* then they said that she had merely copied a Portuguese book, a hundred years old; then they said that the Nunnery was not constructed as Maria had described it, and. that it had no underground passage.

Finally, the priests said that Maria Monk had always been a woman of bad character, a prostitute and a drunkard, and that she had died wretchedly in the insane asylum on Blackwell's Island.

The Romanists allege that Bloody Queen Mary and her

bilious spouse, Philip II. of Spain, were virtuously amiable persons, and that Queen Elizabeth and Martin Luther were tools of the Deivl. The Romanists see may things to admire in the Massacre of St. Bartholomew, and many a good word is being said for the Inquisition. The Romanists are confident that Torquemada and the Duke of Alva had kind hearts, and are certain that the Jesuits did right to murder Henry IV. and the Prince of Orange.

When the Romanist mind takes colors of that kind, *truth* becomes a negligible matter.

What *is* the truth about Maria Monk? A Romanist and a Jesuit—one M. J. Walsh, of Augusta, Georgia—roundly asserted in a recent issue of *The Sunday Visitor,* a leading Catholic paper, that *"There never was a Maria Monk case!"*

Let us examine the record: let us weigh the evidence: let us see whether there ever was a Maria Monk case—a fact which we might easily believe, after we learn that even the Romanists admit that there *was* a Maria Monk.

Too astute and too cowardly to prosecute the Harper Brothers and Maria Monk, the priests took up the weapons of Jesuitism.

A bulky book called "Maria Monk's Daughter," was published in New York by the U. S. Publishing Co.—whatever *that* concern may have been. It was probably a nice, patriotic name to cover a Roman Catholic publisher. In this volume, a "Mrs. L. St. John Eckel," strives to show up *her own mother,* as an imposter and a bawd!

The loyal daughter says in her story that she wrote her book *at the command of a priest.* This admission, of course, puts the royal o. k. on the work.

The Eckel woman asesrts that Maria Monk was Mrs. St. John, and says of her, "She was my mother, *and I hated her."*

The narrative of Mrs. Eckel is so confused, and so very much in contrast to the simple clearness of Maria Monk's, that it is difficult to follow and untangle her statements.

Mrs. Eckel apparently means to be understood as saying that her father and mother were always fussing; that her father perjured himself in the lame effort to steal some property; that his neighbors detested him, and that her mother and he separated, *because* her mother was so much worse than her father. But yet Mrs. Eckel declared that her father was a descendant of Lord Bolingbroke, and had the best blood of Old England in his veins. We must assume then, that Mrs. Eckel "took after" her mother.

Of the pitiable end of Maria Monk, this extraordinay

daughter says, with a pathos of which she appeared to be unconscious:

"At last when my mother was sent to Blackwell's Island, *my sister* would often prevail upon the boatmen to let *her* go over *with the convicts;* and, when she got there, *our* mother would *always* be waiting for *her;* and her first words would be: *'Have you heard from the children? When shall I see them again?"*

No word about yourself, poor Maria Monk! No complaint of your own base treatment and your living death! No: nothing but the mother's wail, heard all round the world, since the day Eve caught the cold form of Abel to her maternal bosom. The old, old cry of Ramah—Rachel weeping for her children!

"When did you hear from my children? When shall I ever see them again?"

The malignant old Jesuit, Cardinal Gibbons, says in his shamelessly lying book:

"God avenged the crime of two and forty boys who mocked the prophet Eliseus by sending wild beasts to tear them to pieces. The frightful death of Maria Monk, the caluminator of consecrated Priests and Virgins, who ended her life a drunken maniac on Blackwell's Island, *proves* that *our* religious institutions are not to me mocked with impunity."

Of course, if Gibbons wants to believe, *literally,* that two little Jewish she-bears ate 42 Jew boys, at one bait, because the boys had reminded Eliseus that he was bald-headed, it is Gibbons' privilege to do it, there being no law against the literal construction of any Biblical allegory, parable, or folk lore. But when the artful Cardinal argues that the Almighty will not permit people to tell the truth on "consecrated Priests and Virgins," I must remind him that no bears, and no drunken mania destroyed Erasmus, Blanco White, Pope Gregory XII., Joseph McCabe, William Crowley, Rev. Justin D. Fulton, Charles Chiniquy, Bishop Manuel Ferrando, ex-Priest P. A. Seguin, Rev. William Hogan, or the inipuitous men who publish The Menace and The Jeffersonian.

There are many omissions in the "Maria Monk's Daughter" which cannot be explained. It is not stated when, where and of what parentage, "mother" was born; it is not stated when, where, and under what circumstances, "mother" was married to St. John; it is not stated when, where, and how "mother" misbehaved herself; it is not stated when, by whom, and what evidence, "mother" was sentenced to Blackwell's Island. It is not stated that the "Daughter" was present when "mother" was tried, nor that the Daughter ever visited the imprisoned mother; nor that the daughter knew when her mother died, how she died, and where she was buried.

It is not stated where, when, and in what circumstances "father" died, although the Daughter was ravenously fond of "father." It is not stated who were the neighbors and the barkeepers who knew of "mother's" dissolute habits.

Great pains are taken to embellish Daughter's book with a picture of her own lovable self, and of several hard-faced, nutcracker aunts of hers; but no picture of father or mother is presented. In fact, there is the strangest avoidance of names, dates, and corroborating incidents, the very things so necessary to be a book of this character.

The mother's narrative was published in 1836; the Daughter's attack, in 1874: the prudent priests and the dutiful Daughter *patiently waited 38 years before assailing the dead.*

A good many witnesses can die, disappear, or be silenced in 38 years. Against the dead woman, were the organizations of the most powerful and criminal church that ever cursed the world: in favor of the dead, there was nothing, save the intrinsic evidences of truth borne in her plain, connected, circumstantial narrative, supplemented by the affidavits of a few persons who knew Maria Monk, but who could not possibly know what had been done to her in the Nunnery.

There is at least one redeeming feature about "Daughter": she paints herself almost as black as she paints "mother." She seems to exult in the fact that she was a hell-cat, that her uncle declared she was possessed of the Devil, that her aunt said she would come to some bad end, and that she separated from *her* husband, Eckel, who appears to have died in consequence of writing a few stanzas of extremely sad, and deplorably bad poetry.

"Daughter's" uncle and aunt were both right: Daughter *was* possessed of a Devil, else she would never have desecrated the grave of her mother; and she *did* come to a bad end, for she flopped to the Roman Catholic Church, and exhibited her asinine qualities by giving her name to one of the falsest books that Rome ever caused to be published.

As I have indicated, there is not a single shred of evidence produced in this vile book to support its statements. No letter of corroboration, no affidavit, no document, no transcript from any record.

It will occur to every intelligent reader, that the very first requisites to such a work as that of "Maria Monk's Daughter," would have been *a transcript of the court sentence which condemned Maria Monk to Blackwell's Island,* and a transcript from the books kept there, to show what became of her. No such documentary evidence has yet been forthcoming. Nor has anyone ever produced an affidavit, from neighbor, bar-keeper, brothel-keeper, or others, to substantiate the charge that Maria Monk was a drunkard and a prostitute.

It must be clear to you that the Harper Brothers did not assume the risks and responsibilities of such a book as the "Awful Disclosures," without having made careful inquiries into her antecedents. If the book had been a tissue of falsehoods, *the Harper Brothers could have been ruined by libel suits and prosecutions.*

It must be equally clear to you that if Maria Monk *afterwards* became a drunkard and a prostitute, her persecutors would have gathered up affidavits by the dozen, *and published them at that time.*

How did they get her into the asylum for the insane? God knows. Read "Hard Cash," and learn how easily it can be done. Probably no day passes that does not see some victim of greed, or of lust, or of revenge put out of sight, to be seen no more of men forever. Some are buried alive in convents, some in brothels, some in lunatic asylums.

Why should any woman, in a book *issued in her life-time,* falsely confess that she had been raped, held in vile relations to priests, and forced to bear the children of fornication? What possible benefit could she hope to obtain by such a relation of her own shame, and such a libellous publication against living persons whose names she gave? *Why did the Mother Superior of the Black Nunnery never dare to prosecute Maria Monk and the Harper Brothers?*

The Romanists are swift enogh to prosecute people who reveal the truth about Roman Catholic thelogy; and they do not deny that what these defendants published *is the truth*: but they did not dare to prosecute Maria Monk, nor the New York publishers of her book. *Why not?*

THEY WERE AFRAID TO FACE HER IN COURT!

They hounded her, with the cowardice and savagery of wolves; they slandered her and isolated her; they terrorized the poor creature so ruthlessly and persistently that her reason gave way, and she *did* die a raving maniac.

For no greater cause, the mind of the Empress Carlotta failed her, when the benevolent Pope Pius IX. coldly, pitilessly, refused to lift a finger to save Maximilian, the Hapsburgh arch-duke whom the Jesuits and Pope Pius had sent to despotize over the Mexicans.

One night, in 1905, I lay very sick in the Victoria Hotel, New York; and my physician, Dr. John H. Girdner, relieved the dreariness of the hours by telling me of the fate of a young German who had followed Frankie Folsome to this country. The unfortunate youth called himself Bauer, and claimed to belong to the lesser nobility of a small Germanic state. He *may* hae been the son of Caroline Bauer, the known mistress of a German prince who lived with her a while in England.

Young Bauer, a fine, intelligent, manly fellow,—had become acquainted with Frankie Folsome in Europe—so he said.

Anyway, he followed her to this country, and became very annoying and obnoxious to Grover Cleveland. The German labored under the delusion that Miss Folsome was his betrothed, and that Mr. Cleveland had unfairly cut him out. He was quite frantic about it, and very importunate in his demands for an interview with his lost lady.

What did Mr. Cleveland do to rid himself of the nuisance? He secured the affidavits of several doctors—three, as I remember —who deposed and swore that the young German was crazy. Immediately, without further proceedings, he was confined at one of the New York institutions for the insane—possibly Blackwell's Island.

Was the man insane? Who knows? But if it is so easy as all that, to bury a stalwart young man alive, when he has annoyed one Protestant family, how much easier is it for the powerful Roman organizations to make way with one troublesome and friendless old woman!

In Ireland and in England the "Awful Disclosures of Maria Monk" created a panic among the papists. They, too, got in motion, and published "the facts" against the "imposter." I have a copy of "The True History of Maria Mork," sponsored by The Catholic Truth Society, of London; and, according to the fly-leaf, 102,000 have been distributed.

The Catholic Truth Society presents an affidavit alleged to have been made by Dr. William Robertson, *a Justice of the Peace.* This medical jurist deposes and says that three men—names not given—brought "a young female" to his house on November 9, 1834, and that the three men said that the young female called herself Maria Monk, and asserted *that Dr. Robertson was her father!*

The three men had seized upon the young female, "on the banks of the canal, near the extremity of the St. Joseph's suburbs, *acting in a manner which induced some people who saw her to think that she intended to drown herself."*

According to the medical J. P., the three mysterious men brought the young female directly to his house from the canal. Further on in his affidavit he makes this statement:

"To remove her from the watch-house, where she was confined with some of the most profligate women of the town, taken up for inbriety and disorderly conduct on the streets, as she could not give a satisfactory account of herself, I, as a Justice of the Peace, *sent her to gaol as a vagrant.*"

Yet he knew that her father had lived in the city and was named W. Monk.

"In the course of a few days she was released from the gaol." Why? If she was in truth a vagabond and her commitment to jail, legal, what caused her release in a few days without any trial?

The medical jurist further deposes that he felt it incumbent on himself to investigate the whereabouts of Maria Monk during the years she claimed to have lived in the Nunnery. This most diligent of Medico-Justices discovered that the summer of 1832 was passed by Maria at William Henry, *where she was in service*: the winter of 1832-3 "she passed in this neighborhood of St. Ours and St. Denis. The accounts given of her conduct that season, corroborate the opinions I had before entertained of her character."

Any affidavits of the employers in whose service she passed the summer? None. Any letter, or signed statement about "her conduct that season"? None. Any names of employer or acquaintances of Maria mentioned? *None.*

That Robertson may have had some woman sent to jail is probable enough, but he took abundant precautions against impeachment as to *Maria Monk,* for he does not name the three men who seized the young female on the canal, he does not furnish a copy of the gaol-book entry, he does not say in whose service the woman was employed, nor does he name a single person that told him of her bad conduct. Indeed, he does not specify what her "conduct" consisted of, but shuns specification by saying it corroborated his *prejudgment.*

Dr. Robertson's testimony—vague as it is and never subjected to cross-examination—*cannot be reconciled with that of Maria Monk's Daughter.* If the one is true, the other is false; and the most charitable view which can be taken of Dr. Robertson's affidavit is, that the "young female" of whom he speaks was not Maria Monk.

Following Dr. Robertson, comes *the mother of Maria Monk,* and her evidence, as published by the Catholic Truth Society, is an amazing contradiction of both Robertson and the "Daughter." The mother's affidavit was taken by Dr. Robertson himself, and is dated *nearly a month ahead of his.* Yet, in his own evidence, the Doctor does not mention Maria's mother, nor any of the alleged facts disclosed by her.

The mother states that in August, 1835, a man named Hoyte

brought her daughter Maria Monk to Montreal, and that Maria then had a child five weeks old. Hoyte and Maria had come from New York and put up at the Goodenough Tavern. Hoyte was a preacher, and he and two other preachers—one named Brewster—endeavored to bribe Maria's mother to swear that Maria had been a nun.

There was a Mrs. Tarbert who testified as follows:

"I knew the said Maria Monk: last spring, she told me that the father of the child she was then carrying was burned in Mr. Owsten's house. Last summer she came back to my lodgings and told me that she had made out the father of her child. The next morning I found that she was in a house of bad fame, where I went for her.

Maria Monk then told me that the father of her child wanted her to swear an oath that would lose her soul forever.

I then told Maria, 'Do not lose your soul for money.' "

Now let us sum up these three affidavits:

In November, 1834, three unnamed men prevent Maria Monk from jumping into the canal, and Dr. Robertson flings her into the calaboose with lewd women, "as a vagrant." Nothing against her can be proved, and she is released in a few days.

In August, 1835, Maria comes to Montreal from New York, with a baby, and a man named Hoyte; and Hoyte, at the instigation of the Devil and his own wicked mind, repeatedly tempts old Mrs. Monk, proposing to protect her for life, if she will swear that Maria had been a nun. St. Bridget fortifies the virtue of old Mrs. Monk, and she says to Hoyte, in effect, "Get behind me, Satan."

Whereupon, the repulsed Hoyte takes Maria, and retires into a suburb of Montreal, where the two (and the baby) dwell together in sinful satisfaction.

In the Spring of 1834, three months before the Hoyte episode, Maria Monk told Mrs. Tarbert that the father of her child (Maria's) got burned in Mr. Owsten's house; and we must assume that he was killed by it. But "last Summer"—which would be June, July or August, Mrs. Tarbert finds Maria in a house of ill fame.

The priests who got up this absurdly jumbled booklet had no skill in the management of evidence, and no gift of critical analysis.

If Mrs. Tarbert meant the Spring and Summer of 1835, she smashes the affidavit of old Mrs. Monk. But if Mrs. Tarbert meant the Spring and Summer of 1834, she smashes that of Dr. Robertson.

In October, 1835, Mrs. Tarbert testified to where Maria

Monk was "last Spring" and "last Summer"; and she puts Maria in a bawdy house in Montreal, *where the Monk family lived.*

When one of us, in October, says "last Spring," or "last Summer," the meaning is generally understood to be, those seasons of *the same year.* In that case, Mrs. Monk is flatly contradicted by Mrs. Tarbert, for if Maria was the inmate of a brothel in Montreal, the Summer of 1835, her mother could not have truthfully sworn that she came from New York, with Hoyte, *the same Summer!*

Besides, a respectable hotel, like Goodenough's, would not have entertained a Montreal courtesan as one of its respectable guests.

There is one fact which *proves* that Mrs. Tarbert meant the Spring and Summer of 1835: *it is the age of the baby!*

Old Mrs. Monk swears that "in August, 1835," the child of Maria *was five weeks old;* and Mrs. Tarbert swears that she knew Maria was with child in the Spring *and Summer.* Then, necessarily, it was the Spring and Summer of 1835.

But *what* was Maria doing in a brothel when so near confinement? and *how* did she go from Montreal to New York, strike up with Hoyte, and reappear at Montreal with a five-weeks baby *in August?*

In the war of affidavits which followed the publication of the "Awful Disclosures," the defenders of the ruined nun, were neither few nor timid. I present the more important testimonials in her behalf:

First, there was a statement signed by seven men certifying that they were acquainted with Maria Monk, and that they believed her revelations as to the Black Nunnery to be true. The signers were W. C. Brownler, John J. Slocum, Andrew Bruce, D. Fanshaw, David Wesson, and Thomas Hogan.

Second, there was the affidavit of William Miller, which follows:

City and County of New York, ss.

William Miller, being duly sworn, doth say: I knew Maria Monk when she was quite a child, and was acquainted with her father's family. My father, Mr. Adam Miller, kept the government school at St. John's, Lower Canada, for some years. Captain William Monk, Maria's father, lived in the garrison a short distance from the village, and she attended the school with me for some months, probably as much as a year. Her four brothers also attended with us. Our families were on terms of intimacy, as my father had a high regard for Captain Monk; but the temper of his wife was such, even at that time, as to cause much trouble. Captain Monk died very suddenly, as was reported, in consequence of being poisoned. Mrs.

Monk was then keeper of the Government House in Montreal, and received a pension which privilege she has since njoyed.

In the summer of 1832, I left Canada, and came to this city. In about a year afterward, I visited Montreal, and on the day when the Governor reviewed his troops, I believe about the end of August, I called at the Government House, where I saw Mrs. Monk and several of the family. I inquired where Maria was and she told me that she was in the nunnery. This fact I well remember, because the information gave me great pain, as I had unfavorable opinions of the nunneries.

On reading the Awful Disclosures, I at once knew she was an eloped nun, but was unable to find her until a few days since, when we recognized each other immediately.

I give with pleasure my testimony in her favor, as she is among strangers, and exertions have been made against her. I declare my personal knowledge of many facts stated in her book and my full belief in the truth of her story, which shocking as it is, cannot appear incredible in those persons acquainted with Canada.

WILLIAM MILLER.

Sworn before me, this 3d day of March, 1836.

BENJ. D. K. CRAIG,
Commissioner of Deeds.

No attempt was ever made to impeach William Miller. In the book of the "Daughter," he is not mentioned, nor is Captain William Monk named at all. The widow, Mrs. William Monk, never returned to contradict Miller; and, yet, he had mentioned the time and place of inquiry concerning the whereabouts of Maria. If the girl had *not* gone to school with Miller as he testified, there would have been no difficulty in proving him a liar, by some of the scholars, or by some member of the garrison.

Third:

AFFIDAVIT OF JOHN HILLIKER.
(From the New York Journal of Commerce.)

"City and County of New York, ss.

"John Hilliker, being duly sworn, doth depose and say that one day early in the month of May, 1835, while shooting near the Third avenue, opposite the three-mile stone, in company with three friends, I saw a woman sitting in a field at a short distance, who attracted our attention. On reaching her, we found her sitting with her head down and could not make her return any answer to our questions. On raising her hat, we saw that she was weeping. She was dressed in an old calico frock (I think of a greenish color), with a checked apron, and an old black bonnet. After much delay and weeping, she began to answer my questions, but not until I had got our companions to leave us, and assured her that I was a married man, and disposed to befriend her.

"She then told me that her name was Maria, that she had been a nun in a Nunnery in Montreal, from which she had made her escape, on account of the treatment she had received from priests in that institution, whose licentious conduct she strongly intimated to me. She mentioned some particulars concerning the Convent and her escape. She spoke particularly of a small room where she used to attend, until the physician entered to see the sick, when she accompanied him to write down his prescriptions; and said that she escaped through a door which he sometimes entered. She added that she exchanged her dress after leaving the Nunnery, and that she came to New York in company with a man, who left her as soon as the steamboat arrived. She further stated that she expected soon to give birth to a child, having become pregnant in the Convent; that she had no friend, and knew not where to find one; that she thought of destroying her life; and wished me to leave her, saying that If I should hear of a woman being drowned in the East River, she earnestly desired me never to speak of her.

"I asked if she had had any food that day, to which she answered no; and I gave her money to get some at the grocery of Mr. Cox, in the neighborhood. She left me; but I afterwards saw her in the fields, going towards the river; and after much urgency prevailed upon her to go to a house where I thought she might be accommodated, offering to pay her expenses. Failing in this attempt, I persuaded her, with much difficulty, to go to the alms-house; and there we got her received, after I had promised to call to see her, as she said she had something of great consequence which she wished to communicate to me, and wished me to write a letter to Montreal.

"She had every appearance of telling the truth; so much so, that I have never for a moment doubted the truth of her story, but told it to many persons of my acquaintance, with entire confidence in its truth. She seemed overwhelmed with grief, and in a very desperate state of mind. I saw her weep for two hours or more without ceasing; and appeared very feeble when attempting to walk, so that two of us supported her by the arms. We observed, also, that she always folded her hands under her apron when she walked, as she described the nuns as doing in her 'Awful Disclosures.'

"I called at the almshouse gate several times and inquired for her, but, having forgotten half of her name, I could not make it understood whom I wished to see, and did not see her until last week. When I saw some of the first extracts from her book in a newspaper, I was confident that they were parts of her story, and when I read the conclusion of the work, I had not a doubt of it. Indeed, many things in the course of the book I was prepared for from what she had told me.

"When I saw her, I recognized her immediately, although she did not know me at first, being in a very different dress. As soon as she was informed where she had seen me, she recognizd me. I have not found in the book anything inconsistent with what she had stated to me when I first saw her.

"When I first found her in May, 1835, she had evidently sought concealment. She had a letter in her hand, which she refused to let me see; and when she found I was determined to remove her, she tore it in small pieces, and threw them down. Several days after I visited the spot again and picked them up, to learn something of the contents, but could find nothing intelligible, except the first part of the signature, 'Maria.'

"Of the truth of her story, I have not the slightest doubt, and I think I never can until the Nunnery is opened and examined.

"JOHN HILLIKER.

"Sworn before me, this 14th day of March, 1835.

"PETER JENKINS,
"Commissioner of Deeds."

The *Protestant Vindicator,* of New York, took up the cause of the persecuted woman, and published *a challenge* to the very priests whose names had been mentioned by Maria Monk. That dare to the Romanists appeared on April 6, 1836.

It was addressed to the Roman Prelate and Priests of Montreal—Messrs. Conroy, Quarter and Schneller, of New York—Messrs. Fenwick and Byrne, of Boston—Mr. Hughes, of Philadelphia—the Arch-Prelate of Baltimore, and his subordinate priests, and also to Bishop England, of Charleston, South Carolina. The terms of the challenge were:

"To meet an investigation of the truth of Maria Monk's 'Awful Disclosures,' before an impartial assembly, over which shall preside seven gentlemen; three to be selected by the Roman priests, three by the executive committee of the New York Protestant Association, and the seventh as chairman to be chosen by the six.

"An eligible place in New York shall be appointed and the regulations for the decorum and order of the meetings with all the other arrangements, shall be made by the above gentlemen.

All communications upon this subject from any of the Roman priests or nuns, either individually, or as delegates for their superiors, addressed to the Corresponding Secretary of the New York Protestant Association, No. 142 Nassau street, New York, will be promptly answered."

This challenge was published for several weeks, and nobody ventured to accept it. Afraid of a show-down, afraid to meet the woman they had so foully wronged, the Romanists slunk back in guilty silence, preferring to trust to their favorite weapons, slanders, abuse, falsehoods, denials, and defamation of character.

What hope of fair treatment could Maria Monk cherish, when her traducers are the same that seek to defile the purity of Martin Luther and his wife?

The challenge of the *Protestant Vindicator* was accompanied by the following editorial:

"THE CHALLENGE.—We have been waiting with no small degree of impatience to hear from some of the Roman priests. But neither they, nor their sisters, the nuns, nor one of their nephews or nieces, have yet ventured to come out. Our longings meet only with disappointment. Did ever any person hear of similar conduct on the part of men accused of the highest crimes, in their deepest dye? Here is a number of Roman priests, as actors, or accessories, openly denounced before the world as guilty of the most outrageous sins against the sixth and seventh commandments. They are charged before the world with adultery, fornication, and murder! The allegations are distinctly made, the place is mentioned, the parties are named, and the time is designated; for it is lasting as the annual revolutions of the seasons. And what is most extraordinary—the highest official authorities in Canada know that all these statements are true,

and they sanction and connive at the iniquity! The priests and nuns
have been offered, for several months past, the most easy and certain
mode to disprove the felonies imputed to them, and they are still as
the dungeons of the inquisition, silent as the deah-like quietude of the
Convent cell; and as retired as if they were in the subterraneous passages between the Nunnery and Lartique's habitation.   Now, we
contend, that scarcely a similar instance of disregard for the opinions
of mankind, can be found since the Reformation, at least, in a Protestant country.   Whatever disregard for the judgment of others,
the Romish priests may have felt, where the inquisition was at their
command, and the civil power was their Jackal and their Hyena; they
have been obliged to pay some little regard to the opinion of Protestants, and to the dread of exposure.   We therefore repeat the
solemn indubitable truth—that the facts which are stated by Maria
Monk, respecting the Hotel Dieu Nunnery at Montreal, are true as the
existence of the priests and nuns—that the character, principles, and
practices of the Jesuits and nuns in Canada are most accurately de-
lineated—that popish priests, and sisters of charity in the United
States, are their faithful and exact counterparts—that many female
schools in the United States, kept by the papist teachers, are nothing
more than places of decoy through which young women, at the most
delicate age, are ensnared into the power of the Roman priests—that
the toleration of the monastic system in the United States and Britain,
the only two countries in the world, in which that unnatural abomina-
tion is now extending its withering influence, is high treason against
God and mankind.   If American citizens and British Christians, after
the appalling developments which have been made, permit the con-
tinuance of that prodigious wickedness which is inseparable from
Nunneries and the celibacy of popish priests, they will ere long ex-
perience that divine castigation which is justly due to transgressors
who wilfully trample upon all the appointments of God, and who
subvert the foundation of national concord and extinguish the com-
forts of domestic society.   Listen to the challenge again! All the
papers with which the Protestant Vindicator exchanges, are requested
to give the challenge one or more than one insertion." (Here it was
repeated.)

Other testimonials purporting to come from schoolmates and
acquaintances of Maria Mank were published, and vouched for
by the *Protestant Vindicator,* which was in possession of the
names of the witnesses; but, as there is no way for me to learn
these names, I exclude that part of the record.

As already stated, the Catholic paper, *Sunday Visitor,* which
has the largest general circulation claimed by any papal organ,
published an extremely bold article by the Jesuit, M. J. Walsh,
roundly denying the Maria Monk story, and affirming that there
never had been *such* a case.   In other words, no woman had *ever*
been wronged in a convent in the manner described by Maria
Monk.

As nunneries have existed for a thousand years, confining·
millions of women in a forlorn state of helplessness, and giving millions of bachelor priests unlimited power over these im-

prisoned women, you will at once realize how comprehensive is the statement of Walsh. If not a single one of those Maria Monks was ever wronged by the unmarried men who had access to them, much false evidence has been given by Popes, Councils, Bishops, priests, monks, Sisters, and Romanist writers.

The Jesuit Walsh cited Appleton's Encyclopedia, wherein Maria Monk, he said, was rated as an impostor. I happened to have a copy of the original edition of that work, issued in the year 1856, *and Maria Monk's name is not mentioned.* It had no right to a place there, for the reason that she is not a historic character. A poor, ruined, flung-adrift nun, hounded by the relentless wolves of Rome—what business had her name in a Cyclopedia of illustrious men and women? None of the biographical dictionaries or encyclopedias mentioned Maria Monk— *until when?* Not until recent years when Rome systematically set to work to re-write history, re-write encyclopedias, re-write school-books, and to even emasculate Protestant literature.

Thus it happens that in 1888, the Appleton Encyclopedia of Biography *does* mention Maria Monk as an impostor. A Romanist writer compiled that libel, and Romanist money no doubt paid for the space it occupies. Even the Encyclopedia Brittanica has knelt to Rome, *and the Jesuits have written thirty of the articles for the 11th edition of that deteriorating work.*

Probably Maria Monk will now figure in the Brittanica, and of course she will appear as an impostor.

In making a reply to Walsh in *The Jeffersonian,* I stated that the Romanists waited for the death of all the•witnesses, before they began to doctor the books, and to deny that there ever was a Maria Monk case. My statement brought forth two letters which show how nearly correct the Romanists were in presuming that Time had mowed down all of those who personally knew the unfortunate victim of the Black Nunnery.

The first is from G. Major Taber, of Los Angeles, California:

My Dear Editor: In your issue of March 9th, I notice that a Jesuit by the name of Walsh claims "There never was a Maria Monk case."

Now, Mr. Editor, if you will courteously allow me to have a friendly chat with the readers of The Jeffersonian, as I desire to present a few facts relating to the above, and being from a personal knowledge and observation, ought to settle the question as to the facts in the above case.

When a young man of eighteen, I travelled through nearly every city and village from Quebec to Ottawa as a Daguerrian artist for over three years, and have taken pictures of dead nuns in their convents.

In 1850 I resided for six months in a village opposite Montreal, where Maria Monk was born, and where her family lived, and I made special inquiry of an old Catholic who had known her from childhood, if Maria Monk had told the truth in her book. His answer was: "There is no doubt about it."

I learned also that when the sewers of the "Hotel Dieu" nunnery were cleaned out, that scores of infant skulls and bones were discovered.

Not only that, but I learned that there was a change made in

A WELL-KNOWN PRIEST.

all of the rooms of the nunnery, in the attempt to disprove the description she had given in her book.

Now, gentle reader, I have no hesitation in claiming that, if this Jesuit Walsh asserts that the "Maria Monk case was a fabrication," he is either an ignoramus or a liar, as I know from personal knowledge from Catholics not long after, and during the year 1850, that she did not misrepresent the facts claimed in her book.

Allow me to state further that when in Montreal at one time I winessed a long string of "Pietists" marching through the street, and because I failed to doff my hat, and bow my head when they passed, a Catholic police scoundrel rapped me on my head with his billy. That's Catholicism. How would you have liked such treatment?

In order for the readers of The Jeffersonian to learn what reliance they may have as to my reliability, allow me to state, with usual modesty, that, although a Northern man, I spent over three years in the employ of Uncle Sam, and five years as a resident of Decatur, Alabama. I purchased the first plantation sold to a Northern man after the war, in 1865, and raised cotton for three years. I know the Southern people well, and they were among my best friends.

While there I wrote articles for the Georgia Cultivator on the history and management of the honey bee. And, more than that, in November, 1777, my grandfather, Thomas Taber, married Hanna Davis, who resided in Vermont with her brother, Timothy Davis, and their cousin, Jefferson Davis, often visited them when a young man. I know to be true, as my oldest brother knew them well.

Pardon me, Mr. Editor, for my long article, for I realize that the efforts, in many respects, of the last three Presidents for political purposes, have catered to a class who are tools to an old "Petticoat" who dares not show himself outside a walled and well-guarded prison.

Los Angeles, Calif. G. MAJOR TABER.

The second is from Captain W. M. Somerville, an old sailor who is now at the Snug Harbor, and whose name was furnished me by Dr. A. P. English, of Jacksonville, Florida:

Sailors' Snug Harbor, New Brighton,
Staten Island, N. Y., March 16, 1916.

Hon. Thomas E. Watson, Thomson, Ga.

Dear Sir: Your communication of the 13th inst. duly received yesterday with enclosure, which I had already read, Dr. English, of Jacksonville, having sent it to me. I am afraid that the Doctor has led you to expect rather too much of me, and rather than dicate what I know of Maria Monk to a stenographer. I will just write it, and if you find anything in it that will be of use to you in this controversy you can have it typewritten and return it to me for attestation.

I married a lady in Montreal in 1862 who was born and brought up beside Maria Monk and her parents in LaPrairie, opposite Montreal, on the south side of the St.Lawrence. She never doubted the truth and correctness of Maria Monk's book. I have it in my home in Florida, and have had it for fifty years, but was always under the impression that it was written by Maria Monk herself. My wife died of yellow fever in Florida in 1888 or I would have consulted her and obtained more definite information of the Monk family. But as far as I recollect, she told me that they were English and Episcopalians, and were in connection with a regiment of British soldiers stationed at that time in LaPrairie.

I knew John Monk, a relative of Maria Monk, who had his office in Little St. James, North Montreal, and was the lawyer for my brother-in-law, C. McAdam, a bookseller of whom I purchased Maria Monk's book. I did not know anything of her daughter, Mrs. Eckel, nor of the last days of Maria Monk, nor of her death. Neither do I know anything of Col. W. L. Stone, nor of his visit to Montreal.

I remember seeing the underground vaults of the Hotel Dieu, on N. Hospice Street, when it was torn down to make room for a nice row of commercial buildings belonging to the nuns, which of course paid no taxes.

When I was sailing to Montreal we used to carry large carboys of vitriol which was said to have been for use by the nuns in destroying the bodies of those novices who refused to surrender their bodies to the lust of the visiting priests. We had to carry such carboys on deck.

I lived seven years in Montreal, and never heard Maria Monk's history questioned, far less denied.

During the summer months there was a woman who made regularly three trips a week to Quebec and brought up four babies in the clothes baskets for the Grey Nunnery, which also had an unlocked gate on McGill M. provided with a receptacle to receive babies from whomsoever might place them in it. The receipt of such strange babies, of course, covered the well-known fact of those born to the nuns of the institution.

St. Piere Island, in the St. Lawrence, above the Victoria Bridge, belonged to the nuns, on which was a large house popularly known as the Breeding Cage, where the nuns were sent for their confinement.

Consecrating the Womb of the Bride.—I can remember when a boy, seven years ago, hearing a highlander from Inverness, Scotland, telling his comrades of having been at a Roman Catholic wedding in a hotel when the priest took the bride to a bedroom upstairs to consecrate her womb before he would perform the marriage ceremony; and when I lived in Ottawa, in 1860, I knew a lumberman who was wealthy, and was commonly reported in his neighborhood to have paid a large sum to the priest to allow him to have his bride to himself.

Yours faithfully,
W. M. SOMMERVILLE.

So much has been said by the Romanists to discredit Maria Monk's statements in regard to secret passages, secret chambers, and secret crimes in the Black Nunnery, that I will lay before you an exact description of the secret rooms of the Inquisition, near the Pope's palace, in Rome—not "the *Spanish* Inquisition," but the Italian. It is taken from Dr. Theodore Dwight's History of the Roman Republic of 1849, Chapter XII.:

The Opening of the Inquisition of Rome.—Feelings of the People on Entering It.—The Edifice.—Its History.—Divisions.

The following account of it is translated from "L'Italia del Popola," and was written by a distinguished writer, F. De Boni, an eye-witness, of what he describes.

Near the Vatican Square, between the Church of St. Peter and the Castle of Saint Angelo, extends a street which bears a melancholy name: "Via della Inquisizione"—The Street of the Inquisition. There that tribunal resides, which makes the altar a stepping-stone to the prison.

In that street multitudes of people daily crowded in March and April of 1849, and passed through the spacious edifice to which it leads, uttering imprecations and maledictions as they returned, then silently dispersed to their homes, with indignation, fear and horror contending in their breasts. Sometimes a shout might be heard, a cry of "Vila la Republica!" and then a hundred voices would reply: for a Viva then expressed, to every heart, a malediction on the past and a hope of the future.

Falsehoods and calumnies have been published respecting this subject. For the sake of truth, then, let us register, in the following pages, the memory of facts, which will afford assistance in tracing the picture of the Italian revolution. Being sure of triumph, we are not impatient. Let us for the present consign over our vengeance to history.

On the 4th of April, 1849, the government of the Republic (that is, the Assembly and Executive power), moved by a sentiment of justice and Christian compassion, having established, on the ruins of the papal tyranny, the legitimate reign of brotherly equality, decreed that the houses of the Holy Office should become the habitations of poor families, who had only miserable dwellings, in unhealthy and confined quarters of Rome. And in order to teach, in a practical manner, that idleness leads to misery, and to cultivate a love of labor, self-respect and self-dependence, the government did not grant the apartments gratuitously, but required the payment of small sums, in amounts and ways within the reach of all, at the end of each month.

They intended thus to cancel, on a republican plan, the remains of ancient tyranny, by consecrating to beneficence what papal severity had devoted to torture.

Consequently the Holy Office, which for three centuries had been closed, except to the victims of suspicion, and the martyrs of liberty and conscience, whom it buried in prison, or gave to the flames, was thrown open to the people. Crowds entered it day after day, and were excited by the deepest emotions, at the terrible spectacle. Within these walls the people took their most solemn abjurations against the clerical orders, and repeated from their hearts the oath against the government of the priests. The people can reason clearly; and, in those religious prisons, they better understood the necessity of rejecting the pastor who bears a sword instead of a crook, and more admired and loved the gentle doctrine of the Nazarene, while shuddering at the tortures inflicted in his name. By seeing the effects of the dominion of the clerical system, they understood the cruelty which had enforced the creed of the Catholic primate in Italy. They saw his hand applying instruments of blood, guided by barbarous zeal, sacrilegious ambition and ignorance. The knowledge of the people is all in the heart. By calling to mind the past, in their imagination, they depicted the horrible scenes which had occured within those walls year after year; felt in their own hearts the agonies endured by men, who had disdained to sell their consciences for the price of their blood, although ignorant of their history and even of their names. With rage and imprecations, they made the circuit of those apartments, prisons and subterranean passages, which had heard so many groans, witnessed so many tears and sorrows, swallowed up so many victims and been the mysterious centre of that universal religious despotism, which, with subtle chains, not yet destroyed, bound down all Europe, and in the latest centuries has sustained civil tyranny. The spectators perhaps sometimes, thinking they were dreaming, and feeling as if not secure, would look behind them, fearing to see a Father Inquisitor appear, and in revenge for their profanation, shut the door of those horrid prisons.

And what awful scenes did history bring up to the mind, to those who passed through those dismal halls.

From this place so near the Vatican, issued the orders for the slaughter of the Jews and the last Mussulmans in Spain. Within this building was decreed the murder of the Waldenses in the Guardia of Lombardy and the Subalpine Vallies; here Galileo was tortured, the imprisonment of Gianone was ordered, Pasquali was condemned to the flames, as well as Carnesecchi, Paleario and Giordano Bruno.   Here were planned the murder of the Ugonotti and the horrors of Flanders. Here the censorship was organized, war was made against the printing press, a holy act was pronounced treason, and attempts were made to chain the mind.   But that Prometheus has now broken its bonds, and the world is going on under its influence.   From this place proceeded the mysterious orders which sent at once, to all parts of Europe, unarmed but formidable legions of men, towards the same object. Here was thrown out an immense net, which confined, in the same meshes the monarch and the peasant; which transformed the wife into the accuser of her husband, the son into the betrayer of his father. Here was, and will soon be again, the whispering gallery of all Europe. But how long shall it last?

He that enters this building, and is not utterly ignorant of history, must be moved with deep emotions, amidst the stench of putrid corpses, and cannot but take an oath for the cause of the people, while he thinks of the humane doctrines of Christ, who pardoned, while dying for his enemies.   We will now endeavor to describe the edifices, as memory enables us, not as they formerly had been, but as they were when seen by the Roman people in the month of April, 1849.

The edifice of the Holy Roman Inquisition was erected in part about the middle of the sixteenth century, of simple and secure architecture, as much as was required by the times, when taste, preserving a trace of the dying popular greatness, was declining. The present remains of it do not show what the interior was in those times, when the imprisonment of Lutherans was demanded.   It is presumed by some, that the edifice rests its walls upon a prison of Nero.

This great fabric may be divided into three parts, having the form of two rectangular buildings and a trapezium united.   The first rectangular part, which fronts the street, originally belonged to a Cardinal; and Pius V. gave it to the Inquisition, who added a number of cells.   It has little ornament on the front, and only two stories, each with a loggiato, or gallery, with columns of the Tuscan order, if my memory is correct.   The second rectangular part, which is constructed in like manner, differs only in being of smaller dimensions and more simple.   It had originally two stories and two galleries; the lower of which, in the former half of the seventeenth century, was shut in to make new prisons, the greater part of the subterranean cells probably being then abandoned.   Perhaps at the same time another story was built, where new prisons were formed, the only ones which in our age have received prisoners, in this second rectangle. The remaining part, served in all probability, for the family of the Holy Office, where no other persons could enter.   This third part remained incomplete, wanting the left wing; and the right wing is not finished.   A high wall extends transversely, to exclude from human view the horrid mysteries which, for three centuries, were performed in that populous tomb.

In the month of March (1849), the government of the Republic ordered accomodations for stables for the national artillery, and appropriated a part of the Inquisition, under the closed gallery of the second court.   There the Father Inquisitor, a Dominican, resided, whom in the great fervor of disdain, no one offended. He offered no other resistance to the will of the Government, but a protest; and he was allowed to protect. In order to obtain a place to stable the horses, a space was opened in the walls; when the workmen discovered an aperture. The ardent curiosity which had always, up to that time, surrounded everything relating to the Holy Office, and the hatred against the government of the priests, suspended their labors. The rubbish was removed, they descended into a small subterranean place, damp, without light or passage out, with no floor but a blackish oleagenous earth resembling that of a cemetery. Here and there scattered about pieces of garments, of ancient fashions—the clothes of unfortunate persons, who had been thrown down from above, and died of wounds, or hunger. A baiocco (or penny) of Pius 7th, was picked up, which probably denotes the epoch when that abode of darkness and despair was walled up. The rich soil had hardly begun to be removed, before human bones were uncovered in some places, with some very long locks of hair, which had doubtless ornamented the heads of females. The hands trembled, as well as the hearts of those who went on to uncover and collect those funeral reliques. What temples had been shaded by those tresses? what opinions had been their crime? who had sent spies to seize these victims? who can answer the questions? who will ever be able? Poor martyrs of ignorance and fanaticism, torn perhaps from the mother's arms to be thrown into a cloister, and from the cloister into such a dungeon, without light or door; still young and beautiful! These locks of hair were dishevelled in their agonies of death, and there they expired, disconsolate, forgotten by the world, without a kiss from a friend, without receiving a sigh or a tear, or even a handful of dust upon their corpses.

Many of the spectators carried away pieces of the earth and hair, as amulets against the tyranny of the Pope. It is certain that the "Trap-door" swallowed victims of whom it was important to the Holy Office to destroy all traces, because the Foro, or Judgment-hall is over it, in the second story of the first edifice, and it is exactly under the vestibule of the chamber of the "Second Father Companion," which adjoined the Hall of the Tribunal.

The other modern prisons are contiguous to the last court, which has been converted into a garden. Each of those prisons is a very small cell, capable of containing only a single person, being in two stories and all alike. They are accessible from an exceedingly narrow corridor, like the cells of a convent. The walls of this passage are everywhere covered with pictures, and inscriptions commenting upon them, which intimate the horrid nature of the institution and hold up to view the severest dogmas of the Catholic religion, not interpreted in a spirit of forgiveness. So well does the Court of Rome know how to confine pardon to heaven. At every step, and near every door, the solemn figure of Christ confronts you, not painted according to representations of the Gospel,—not as if affected more by sympathizing sorrow for men than for himself: but in correspondence with the system of the Inquisition, as if threatening from the cross. On every side are scripture passages and mottos, which sentence to eternal flames the hardened sinner. Yet the most tremendous inscriptions were erased after the flight of the Pope.

There, where the French government has placed the correctional prisoners, monks and friars had prisons in the Holy Office. The cells were furnished with beds; and there the greatest disorder and filth everywhere prevailed. Here and there were worn-out cushions, coverlets, chairs and tables, and old clothes of prisoners who died in the cells many years ago. In a certain very small cell were things which indicated horrible secrets: a piece of a woman's handkerchief, of large size, and an old bonnet of a girl about ten years old. Poor little child! What offence, perhaps unknown to you, could it have been, which threw you into the place and destroyed the innocent peace of your infantile years; which taught you to weep in the season of smiles, and perhaps deprived you of your dear and early life. In another cell were found four sandals, and several nuns' cords, a little spindle, caskets containing needles, crucifixes, and unfinished stockings, with the knitting-needles still well-pointed, and an infant's coach.

And so, in almost every one of the prison-rooms were to be seen clothes, ornaments and other relics of their former occupants; and as everything was wrapt in deep and mournful mystery, the imaginations of the people recalled ancient tragical stories, and they wept over the misfortunes of persons of whose names they were ignorant.

The walls of all the cells were covered with inscriptions, some of which expressed despairing grief, but most of them resignation, even in that abode, and under the sufferings inflicted there, so well fitted to becloud the mind, to terrify the boldest heart and to bend the most iron will.

Under the two courts subterranean apartments abounded, communicating with each other. A few only were solitary; and to those there was only one way of access, viz., a trap-door, which denoted death! Some of them were prisons at first, and afterwards converted into store-rooms. To their ceilings were still fastened iron rings which formerly served to give to the Question (torture!) and afterwards to suspend provisions. In one cell on the ground floor, in the second building, a square piece of marble was observed in the floor, which looked like the cover of a hole. It was raised, and beneath was a vault, which proved to be a Vade in pace (go in peace— that is, a place of silent death). Not a ray of light ever could have entered, except when that funeral marble was lifted for a moment, and then it soon again fell, over the head of the condemned person, who was left to die of hunger, in the cold and darkness, and amidst a stillness unbroken unless by his own cries or prayers.

A portion of those subterraneous apartments were closed in the present century, or near the close of the last, as was plainly discovered by a careful examination of the walls, that had shut them in, which had been artificially colored with a grayish hue, to make them look old. This artifice was accidentally discovered.

The rubbish having been removed in one place, indications of a stone staircase were observed, which was cleared, and persons went down thirty steps. At the bottom was found a small chamber, filled up with a mixture of earth and lime, and which proved to be but the first of many others like it. The prisons of Pope Pius V. were now at last discovered. Along the walls were recesses, hollowed out, so formed and arranged as to bring to mind the ancient Columbari or dovecotes. There, it appeared, from what was observed, the condemned were buried alive, being immersed in a kind of mortar up to their necks. In some instances it was evident, they had died slowly and of hunger. This was inferred from the position of the bodies, which people, in great numbers, had come to view this most horrible abode: and marks were seen in the earth of movements made in the conclusive agonies of the last moments, to free themselves from the tenacious mortar, while it was closing round their limbs. The bodies were placed in lines, opposite each other. The skulls were all gone; but these were afterwards found in another place.

APPENDIX A.

Theod. de Niem. Nemor Unionis. Labyrinthus Tract vi, c 34.

Nuper ad nostrum pervenit auditum, quod in partibus Frisiae XXII Monasteria Ordinis S. Benedictu Bremensis, Monasteriensis et Trajectensis dioeceseos consistunt, in quibus olim--tantummodo moniales dicti ordinis degebant, sed successu temporis contigit, quod in eisdem etiam mares ejusdem professionis in magno—numero qualitercunue cum—monialibus—degerent, prout degent ad proesens—in quibus (monasteriis) pene omnis religio et observentia dicti ordinis, ac Dei timor abscessit, libido et corruptio carnis interipsos mares et moniales, necnon alia multa mala, excessus et vitia, quae pudor est effari, per singlua succreverunt—. Fornicantur etiam quam plures hujusmodi monialium cum eisdem sius praelatis monachis et conversis et iisdem monasteriis plures parturiunt filios et filias.—Filios atuem in monachos, et filias taliter conceptas quandoque in moniales dictorum monasteriorum recipi faciunt et procurant; et quod miserandum est, nonnullae ex hujusmondi monialibus materne pietatis oblitae, ac mala malis accumulando aliquos foetus eorum mortificant, et infantes in lucem reditos trucidant * * * Insuper quasi singulre moniales hujusmodi sinqulis monachis et conversis * * * ad instar ancillarum seu uxorum * * * sternent lectos, lavant etiam eis capita et pannos * * * nec non decoquent ipsis cibaria delicata, as die noctuque cum ipsis monachis et conversis in commessationibus et ebrietalibus creberrimt conservantur. Niem Basil, 1566.

(Nuns and Nunneries, p. 184.)

APPENDIX B.

Concilium Moguntiacense. X. Ut clericis interdicatur, mulieres in domo suo habere, omnimodis decernimus. Quamvis enim sacri canones quasdam personas foemi—narum simul cum clericis in una domo habitare permittant; tamen, quod multum dolendum est, saepe audivimus, par illam consessionem plurima scelera esse commissa, ita ut quidam sacerdotum cum propriis soforibus concugbentes, filos ex eis generassent. Et idcirco constituit haec sancta sypodus, ut nullus presbyter ullam foemimum secum in domo propri permittat, quantenus occasio malde suspicionis vel facti lriqui penitus auteratur.

Sacrosanta Concilia Stud.

P. Labbei et G. Cossart, Venice 1728-32, Tom XI, col. 586.

4th DEGREE OATH

OF THE

KNIGHTS OF COLUMBUS

(New Print)

By THOS. E. WATSON

The demand for this 48 page pamphlet has been so great that we have printed a new edition. Mr. Watson in this booklet proves that a person taking this degree is guilty of treason to his country and should be deported. 48 pages of dynamic fire against the Hierarchy.

Price 35c, Delivered

THE TOM WATSON BOOK CO.

THOMSON, GEORGIA

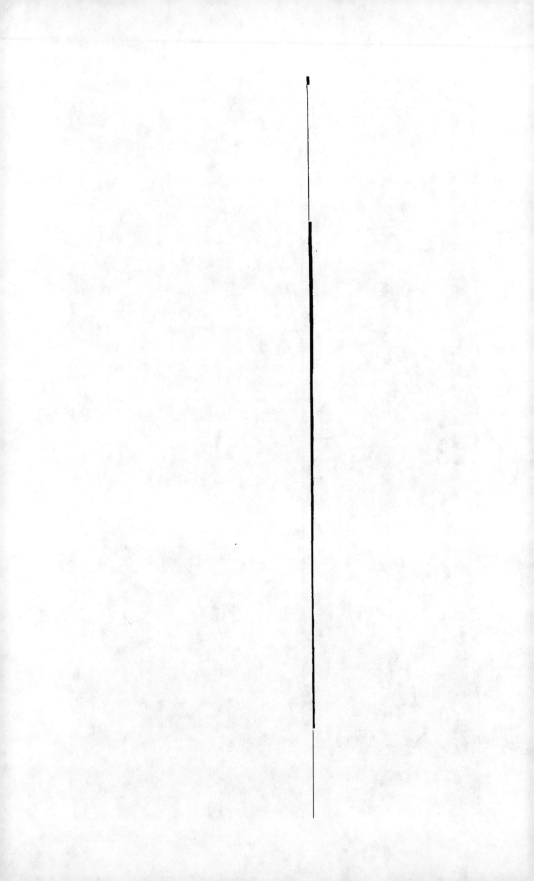

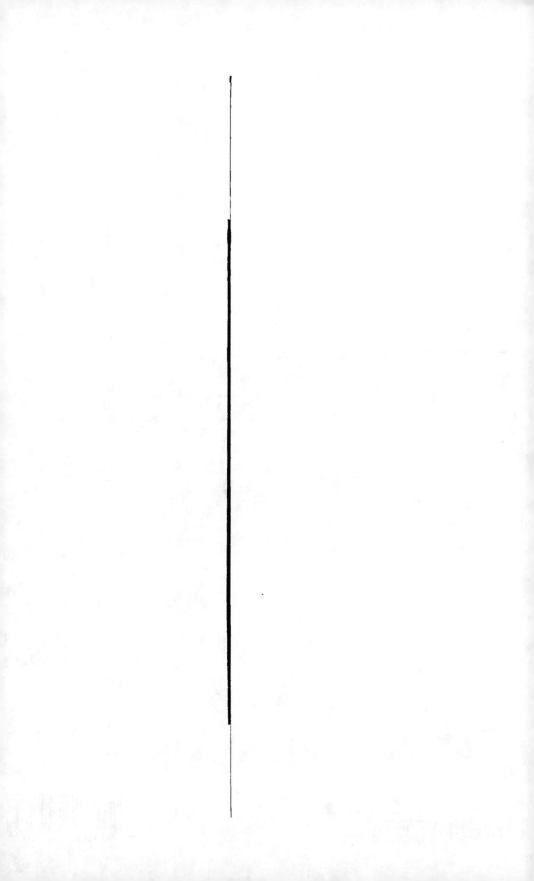

Printed in the USA
CPSIA information can be obtained
at www.ICGtesting.com
LVHW011048130823
755079LV00013BC/487